John Reynolds

Cambridge

NEW EDITION

**checkp●int
English**

1

Workbook

HODDER
EDUCATION
AN HACHETTE UK COMPANY

Answers to many of the exercises can be found at www.hoddereducation.com/checkpoint extras.

This text has not been through the Cambridge endorsement process.

The publishers would like to thank the following for permission to reproduce copyright material:

Text credits

p.3 'How to Travel on a Limited Budget' from www.hostelbookers.com/article/travel-tips; **p.9** Emma Gass, 'As dead as a...' a passage about Dodo from www.go2africa.com/africa-travel-articles/life-after-the-dodo-conservation-in-mauritius (7 April 2009) © 2009 Go2Africa; **p.11** 'The Lost Pirate City of Port Royal', based on article from www.helium.com; **p.12** Mary Seacole, from *Adventures of Mrs Seacole in Many Lands*; **p.15** Laurie Lee, from *I Can't Stay Long* (Penguin Books, 1977); **p.34** 'Boulogne-sur-Mer – Description 1' from website http://bigmikeh.hubpages.com/hub/boulogne-sur-mer-france; **p.44** 'The Man, the Boy and the Donkey' from www.aesopfables.com/cgi/aesop1.cgi?sel&TheMantheBoyandtheDonkey; **p.46** 'King of the Birds', retold by Brishti Bandyopadhyay from www.pitara.com/talespin/folktales/online.asp?story=43; **p.52** Mo McAuley, from 'The Tidy Drawer' from www.eastoftheweb.com/short-stories/Ubooks/TidyDraw.shtml; **pp.54 and 57** Mike Krath, 'High and Lifted Up' from www.eastoftheweb.com/short-stories/Ubooks/HighLift.shtml, reproduced by permission of the author; **p.65** from 'Build a House from Recycled Products' (The Guides Network); **pp.67 and 70:** 'Cow's Head', retold by S.E.Schlosser from http.//americanfolklore.net/folklore/2010/07/cows_head.html, copyright 2010. All rights reserved; **p.77** Philip Waddell, 'Important Notice' from *The Works 2: Poems on Every Subject and for Every Occasion*, edited by Brian Moses and Pie Corbett (Macmillan Children's Books, 2002); **p.78** Pie Corbett, 'The Last Wolf Speaks from the Zoo' from *The Works 2: Poems on Every Subject and for Every Occasion*, edited by Brian Moses and Pie Corbett (Macmillan Children's Books, 2002)

Every effort has been made to trace all copyright holders, but if any have been inadvertently overlooked the publishers will be pleased to make the necessary arrangements at the first opportunity.

Hachette UK's policy is to use papers that are natural, renewable and recyclable products and made from wood grown in sustainable forests. The logging and manufacturing processes are expected to conform to the environmental regulations of the country of origin.

Orders: please contact Bookpoint Ltd, 130 Milton Park, Abingdon, Oxon OX14 4SB. Telephone: (44) 01235 827827. Fax: (44) 01235 400454. Lines are open 9.00–5.00, Monday to Saturday, with a 24-hour message answering service. Visit our website at www.hoddereducation.com.

© John Reynolds 2013
First published in 2013 by
Hodder Education, an Hachette UK Company,
338 Euston Road
London NW1 3BH

Impression number   5 4 3 2
Year   2016 2015 2014 2013

Cover photo © Photo Alto/Laurence Mouton
Typeset in Palatino Light 10.5/12.5 by Integra Software Services Pvt. Ltd., Pondicherry, India
Printed by CPI Group (UK) Ltd, Croydon, CRO 4YY

A catalogue record for this title is available from the British Library

ISBN 978 1444 18444 0

Contents

# Introduction

Welcome to *Cambridge Checkpoint English Workbook 1*. This is the first of three books intended to provide practice in the skills you have acquired by using the *Checkpoint English* series of student's books. Each of the workbooks is planned to complement the corresponding student's book and to support the material contained in it.

The chapters in *Workbook 1* reflect the topics contained in *Student's Book 1*. Each chapter contains two passages illustrating a particular genre of writing with questions to test your understanding of both the content of the passages and your appreciation of the ways in which writers use language to create effects and to entertain their readers. Each chapter also contains exercises to allow you to practise a range of key skills in the use of English which, in general, follow the sequence of the advice given on these key skills in *Student's Book 1*.

This workbook is intended both to help you acquire the skills to be fully competent in your ability to understand and write English and also to act as valuable support in your preparation for the Cambridge Checkpoint Tests that you may take during your school career. There is no set way to approach using the workbook – you may wish to use it to supplement your understanding as you work through each chapter of the student's book or you may prefer to use it to recap on particular topics at a later point. It is hoped that the organisation of the material in the book is sufficiently flexible to allow whichever approach is best suited to an individual's needs.

The following passage is a piece of factual writing. Read it carefully and then answer the questions that follow.

Reading

The Channel Tunnel

Plans for an undersea tunnel joining Britain and France were first drawn up by a French engineer, Albert Mathieu, in 1802. The idea was to transport passengers by horse-drawn carriage. However, as hostilities developed between Britain and France the idea was dropped.

Nevertheless, people still thought about the possibility throughout the nineteenth and twentieth centuries. After the invention of the railway, much thought was given to building a rail tunnel but as early trains were pulled by steam-powered locomotives there were significant practical problems with this idea, as well as the continuing fear that such a tunnel could be used for hostile invasions of both countries.

In the early 1870s, however, the Channel Tunnel Company Ltd started to dig shafts for a tunnel but the project was abandoned in 1875 when there was a change of UK government.

A hundred years later, in the early 1970s, work started again but was abandoned for economic reasons. At last, in 1985, it was finally agreed that the project would go ahead but would be funded privately and not by taxpayers. Various proposals were put forward both for road and rail tunnels and for different types of bridges. The outcome was that a rail tunnel, to be built by the Channel Tunnel Company, was chosen and construction began in 1988.

The tunnel was to run from Folkestone in South East England to Coquelles in Northern France. There would be two rail tunnels plus a central service tunnel. The project involved over 1500 workers and the total cost was around £4650 million (about $7 billion).

> The two ends of the tunnel finally met in 1990 and the tunnel was completed and opened on 6 May 1994. It carries both High Speed passenger trains (London to Paris and Brussels), shuttles for cars and passengers and freight. All are electrically powered. At 23.5 miles (37.5 kilometres) in length, the Chunnel, as it is known, is the longest undersea tunnel in the world.

Now answer these questions. You should try to use your own words in your answers as much as possible.

1 For what reason was the tunnel planned in 1802 abandoned?

_____

2 Suggest a reason why a rail tunnel was thought to be impractical in the nineteenth century.

_____

3 In what way were the proposals for building the Channel Tunnel in 1985 different from those made in the 1970s?

_____

4 How many tunnels were eventually constructed? _____

5 From the final paragraph what do you learn about the way in which the tunnels were constructed?

_____

6 Explain the meaning of the following words and phrases as used in the passage:

  a) hostilities _____

  b) significant practical problems _____

  c) hostile _____

  d) various proposals _____

  e) outcome _____

7 State five facts given in the passage about the Channel Tunnel. **You should refer to the last three paragraphs only.**

a) _____

b) _____

c) _____

d) _____

e) _____

Here is a piece of factual writing from the 'Hostelbookers' website. Read it carefully and then answer the questions that follow.

How to Travel on a Limited Budget

The words 'cheap travel' can conjure up nightmare images of unreliable tour packages and cowboy hoteliers. And, for the unwary, this could indeed become reality, but it really needn't be the case for travellers on a budget!

With a little forward planning, you will find that less can indeed be more in the world of cheap travel; a bit of extra cash in your pocket can mean another week (or even two) of travels and adventures.

The number one rule when it comes to cheap travel is to do some homework and plan ahead. The biggest costs of travelling will be transport and accommodation, and it follows that this is also where the biggest savings can be made.

Booking in advance with budget airlines can save huge amounts, as can checking dates (and times) around your preferred time of travel to find the cheapest; airlines adjust prices according to demand and a flexible schedule can be a great way to find a great deal.

Accommodation prices are also often subject to variation; particularly depending where you book. Websites such as 'Hostelbookers' allow travellers to compare hostel prices quickly and find the best value options for cheap travel. Moreover, there's no additional booking fee charged on the price of a bed!

Hostels and cheap hotels can change their prices at any time so it can pay to book early, especially during the peak season. Conversely, prices can drop at the last minute, but usually only out of season.

However, there's more to cheap travel than booking and research from home. Once you're on foreign soil, the best bet is to find some local secrets, especially when it comes to eating and drinking. Don't be afraid to ask friendly locals, other travellers or the staff at your hostel for tips.

Sticking to a budget on your travels needn't hamper your trip; in fact, it can be an advantage. Staying around the spots geared towards tourism (and paying for the guidebook's 'top' attractions) can mean missing out on a real, authentic taste of the country or city where you're travelling. And stepping off the beaten track to find those low prices can be both exciting and rewarding!

Now answer these questions. You should try to use your own words in your answers as much as possible.

1   Explain what the writer means by these phrases:

   a) nightmare images _____

   b) unreliable tour packages _____

   c) cowboy hoteliers _____

2   According to paragraph 4, why is it important to check dates and times of travel?

   _____

3   Why should you use websites such as 'Hostelbookers'?

   _____

4   What three groups of people should be consulted for advice once you are in a foreign country?

   a) _____

   b) _____

   c) _____

5   Explain what is meant by 'spots geared towards tourism'. Why should you avoid such spots?

   _____

6 In the first column of the table, list the different pieces of advice given in the passage about how to travel cheaply. In the second column, state what can be gained by following these tips.

You should use only information given in the passage and answer using your own words. Try to list the points as concisely as possible.

Budget travel advice	Benefits

7 Compare the way the two passages 'The Channel Tunnel' and 'How to Travel on a Limited Budget' set out to give information. In particular, you should consider the tone of the passages, the language used and the audiences at which you think each was aimed.

_____

_____

_____

_____

_____

_____

Writing task

Write a one-page information leaflet for students joining your school. The leaflet's purpose is to help them in their first week at their new school and it should contain only **facts**. You should include information about: times of the school day; getting around the school; what happens at break and lunch times; key school rules, and so on.

Plan your work in the space below and then write your answer on separate paper.

Exercises

Fact or opinion?

One thing to consider when you are reading a piece of factual writing is whether or not everything that looks like fact actually is a fact. Is it a fact that can be proved or is the writer presenting opinion as fact in order to make his or her argument sound more convincing?

For example:

- 'In the 2010 soccer World Cup Final, Spain beat the Netherlands by 1–0.' This is a **fact** as there is plenty of evidence (television recordings, newspaper reports, and so on) that this is true.

- 'The Spanish team that won the World Cup in 2010 is the greatest soccer team of all time.' This is an **opinion** as it is not possible to prove that this team was better than any other side that has ever played soccer.

- 'Statements made by many experts confirm that the Spanish World Cup winners of 2010 were the greatest soccer team there has ever been.' You need to think about this one. The language introducing the comment makes it sound as if it is a true fact, but all it is really stating is that many experts have **said this**. It is still not possible to prove that this was the greatest ever team and so the point remains the experts' **opinion**.

Read the following statements. Decide whether each one is fact or opinion and then write **F** (for fact) or **O** (for opinion) in the boxes.

1 Nelson Mandela was appointed as President of South Africa on 10 May 1994.

2 The Amazon is the longest river in South America.

3 Basketball is the most exciting sport of all.

4 It is understood that eating an apple a day keeps you healthy.

5 *Titanic* won the Best Film Oscar in 1997.

6 Leonardo di Caprio was undoubtedly the star performer in *Titanic*.

7 The square root of 144 is 12.

8 In time, scientists will be able to prove how the universe was formed.

9 Life on Earth would not exist without water.

10 Many scholars have said that *Hamlet* is the greatest play written by Shakespeare.

You may find it helpful to discuss some of these statements with other members of your group once you have made your own decisions about them.

Parts of speech: nouns and verbs

1   Remind yourself of the definitions of these types of nouns:

-   common nouns
-   proper nouns
-   collective nouns
-   abstract nouns.

Identify each noun used in the following paragraph and write it in the correct column in the table below.

> It was Thursday, a normal day at school. Rohan and Shivane were in their classroom waiting for English, their favourite lesson, to begin. It was the last lesson before the morning recess. The class were reading a novel entitled *Emil and the Detectives* which they were all enjoying. It was full of suspense and excitement. The book was originally written in German and was set in Berlin, the capital city of the country. Rohan had been reading the book on the bus as he travelled to school that morning. He wanted to be a detective when he was an adult. He told Shivane of this ambition. She laughed and said that she liked the book because it told her about life and society in another country in an earlier time. She wanted to travel to Europe when she was older.

Common nouns	Proper nouns	Collective nouns	Abstract nouns

2 Read the following paragraphs and identify all the verbs and their subjects. Then complete the table below. (Some sentences have more than one verb.)

The comical-looking Dodo is probably the first thing people think of when they are asked about the wildlife of Mauritius and, as everyone knows, that unfortunate, flightless bird became famously extinct within a few decades of European settlement.

Not only were they ridiculously easy to catch for the pot, but rats introduced from the settlers' boats soon devoured the eggs and young of the rotund, hapless bird – and rats, mice, shrews and mongooses are still a major threat to Mauritian wildlife today.

Because Mauritius was a completely uninhabited island, untouched by humans and floating in the middle of the Indian Ocean for so long, it is not surprising that there are numerous creatures found there that exist nowhere else in the world. Many of them met the same fate as the poor Dodo and others came very, very close, but hard-working people with incredible foresight saved them from extinction.

Subject	Verb

Sentence types

Read these sentences and decide what type of sentence each one is. Then tick the correct box.

1 We played football after school.

Simple ☐　Compound ☐　Complex ☐

2 The teacher was not impressed with my assignment.

Simple ☐　Compound ☐　Complex ☐

3 As soon as the game was finished, I hurried home for my supper.

Simple ☐　Compound ☐　Complex ☐

4 Rohan always walks to school, but is never late for his lessons.

Simple ☐　Compound ☐　Complex ☐

5 If you lend me your book, I promise to return it as soon as I have finished reading it.

Simple ☐　Compound ☐　Complex ☐

6 Although the traffic was heavy, the bus brought us to school on time.

Simple ☐　Compound ☐　Complex ☐

7 There was mud everywhere, on the carpet, on the chairs and on my shoes.

Simple ☐　Compound ☐　Complex ☐

8 Rohan practised hard every night and hoped to make the First Team in the future.

Simple ☐　Compound ☐　Complex ☐

9 We were late for school as the bus could not get through the traffic jam resulting from the accident that happened earlier in the morning.

Simple ☐　Compound ☐　Complex ☐

10 Shivane, Rohan and I had to explain our lateness to the Headteacher.

Simple ☐　Compound ☐　Complex ☐

Punctuation: full stops and capital letters

The following passage is taken from a history of Port Royal, the famous haunt of Caribbean pirates. However, all the full stops have been removed.

1   Read the passage carefully and insert full stops and capital letters where you think they should go.

2   This passage originally consisted of two paragraphs. Decide where the first paragraph ends and the second begins. Then mark this place in the text with a line or highlighter.

One of the most famous pirates to have his base at Port Royal was Sir Henry Morgan many called him 'the Pirate King', as he amassed a great fortune as well as respect from his many sea battles and raiding ventures however, once he was knighted by the English king, Charles II, he tried to make the region more respectable by attempting to remove the criminals he began to hunt down his old pirate buddies and hanged them at Gallows Point it would be at Morgan's hands that the streets of Port Royal and the story of the pirates would for ever change eventually he was made Governor of Jamaica nevertheless, Port Royal continued as a thriving harbour town, the wealthiest in the Caribbean the Governor of Jamaica made his residence there, hundreds of ships came and went, and large sugar plantations sprang up across the island fate, however, would not let this prosperity continue on 7 June 1692 shortly before noon the earth moved a massive earthquake rocked the island and Port Royal, out there on the end of its spit of land, was destroyed in a matter of moments over half the town simply collapsed and disappeared, sinking into Kingston Harbour as the sandy ground liquefied beneath it over 2000 people were killed instantly, with two or three thousand more dying of injuries, illness and aftershocks the queen city of the Caribbean was shattered as much of it was swallowed up by the sea

Teacher comments

Autobiography

Reading

Mary Seacole was a Jamaican nurse who lived in the nineteenth century and spent much of her life in Europe, where she practised her medical skills. In particular she played a significant role in treating wounded soldiers during the Crimean War (1853–1856) and became highly thought of in English society.

The passage below is taken from the opening pages of her autobiography. Read it carefully and then answer the questions that follow.

Extract 1: Mary Seacole

It is not my intention to dwell at any length upon the recollections of my childhood. My mother kept a boarding-house in Kingston, and was, like very many of the Creole women, an admirable doctress; in high repute with the officers of both services, and their wives, who were from time to time stationed at Kingston. It was very natural that I should inherit her tastes; and so I had from early youth a yearning for medical knowledge and practice which has never deserted me.

When I was a very young child I was taken by an old lady, who brought me up in her household among her own grandchildren, and who could scarcely have shown me more kindness had I been one of them; indeed, I was so spoiled by my kind patroness that, but for being frequently with my mother, I might very likely have grown up idle and useless. But I saw so much of her, and of her patients, that the ambition to become a doctress early took firm root in my mind; and I was very young when I began to make use of the little knowledge I had acquired from watching my mother, upon a great sufferer – my doll. I have noticed always what actors children are. If you leave one alone in a room, how soon it clears a little stage; and, making an audience out of a few chairs and stools, proceeds to act its childish griefs and blandishments upon its doll. So I also made good use of my dumb companion; and whatever disease was most prevalent in Kingston, be sure my poor doll soon contracted it. I have had many medical triumphs in later days, and saved some valuable lives; but I really think that few have given me more real gratification than the rewarding glow of health which my fancy used to picture stealing over my patient's waxen face after long and precarious illness.

Before long it was very natural that I should seek to extend my practice; and so I found other patients in the dogs and cats around me. Many luckless brutes were made to simulate diseases which were raging among their owners, and had forced down their reluctant throats the remedies which I deemed most likely to suit their supposed complaints.

Mary Seacole

Now answer these questions. You should try to use your own words in your answers as much as possible.

1   Explain the meaning of the following words and phrases as used in the passage:

a) inherit her tastes _____

b) yearning _____

c) patroness _____

d) blandishments _____

e) prevalent _____

f) gratification _____

g) my fancy used to picture _____

h) precarious _____

i) simulate _____

2 According to paragraph 2 what did the writer gain from the old lady and what problem might have developed from this?

_____

_____

3 On whom did the writer say she first practised her medical skills?

_____

4 Explain, using your own words, the two sentences 'I have noticed always what actors … upon its doll.'

_____

_____

5 In what ways did the writer extend her practice?

_____

6 What evidence can you find in this passage that it was written over 150 years ago? In your answer you should refer closely to the details contained in the passage and the language used by the writer.

_____

_____

_____

_____

_____

_____

_____

The next passage was written by the English poet and writer Laurie Lee (1914–1997), who wrote two volumes of autobiography, *Cider with Rosie* and *As I Walked Out One Midsummer Morning*.

In the passage below he questions how far any autobiographical account can ever be said to be actually true. Read the passage carefully and then answer the questions that follow.

Extract 2: I Can't Stay Long

Which brings me to the question of truth, of fact, often raised about autobiography. If dates are wrong, can the book still be true? If facts err, can feelings be false? One would prefer to have truth both in fact and feeling (if either could ever be proved). And yet ... I remember recording some opinions held by my mother which she had announced during a family wedding. 'You got your mother all wrong,' complained an aunt. 'That wasn't at Edie's wedding, it was Ethel's.'

Ours is a period of writing particularly devoted to facts, to a fondness for data rather than divination, as though to possess the exact measurements of the Taj Mahal is somehow to possess its spirit. I read in a magazine recently a profile of Chicago whose every line was a froth of statistics. It gave me a vivid picture, not so much of the city, but of the author cramped in the archives.

In writing autobiography, especially one that looks back at childhood, the only truth is what you remember. No one else who was there can agree with you because he has his own version of what he saw. He also holds to a personal truth of himself, based on an indefatigable self-regard. One neighbour's reaction, after reading my book, sums up this double vision: 'You hit off old Tom to the life,' he said. 'But why d'you tell all those lies about me?'

Seven brothers and sisters shared my early years, and we lived on top of each other. If they all had written of those days, each account would have been different, and each one true. We saw the same events at different heights, at different levels of mood and hunger – one suppressing an incident as too much to bear, another building it large around him, each reflecting one world according to the temper of his day, his age, the chance heat of his blood. Recalling it differently, as we were bound to do, what was it, in fact, we saw? Which one among us has the truth of it now? And which one shall be the judge? The truth is, of course, that there is no pure truth, only the moody accounts of witnesses.

But perhaps the widest pitfall in autobiography is the writer's censorship of self. Unconscious or deliberate, it often releases an image of one who could never have lived. Flat, shadowy, prim and bloodless, it is a leaf pressed dry on the page, the surrogate chosen for public office so that the author might survive in secret.

Laurie Lee

Now answer these questions. You should try to use your own words in your answers as much as possible.

1 Explain the meaning of the following words and phrases as used in the passage:

a) If facts err, can feelings be false? _____

_____

b) divination _____

c) the author cramped in the archives _____

_____

d) indefatigable _____

e) suppressing _____

f) censorship of self _____

g) prim _____

h) surrogate _____

2 What is the particular concern expressed by the writer in the first paragraph of the passage?

_____

_____

3 What point is the author explaining by his reference to the 'exact measurements of the Taj Mahal'?

_____

4 How is this point further illustrated by the mention of the magazine article about Chicago?

_____

5 What reasons does the writer give for each of his brothers and sisters remembering the same event differently?

_____

_____

6 By referring closely to the lines from 'The truth is, of course …' (the last sentence of paragraph 4) to the end of the passage, explain **a)** why the writer thinks that 'there is no pure truth' and **b)** what he thinks about how authors of autobiographies portray themselves.

a) _____

_____

b) _____

_____

7 Make a list of the main points made by the writer of this passage about the problems of writing autobiography. How far do you think that they are reflected in Extract 1, written by Mary Seacole?

Problems:

_____

_____

_____

_____

In Extract 1:

_____

_____

_____

_____

Writing task

Write an autobiographical account entitled 'A Family Holiday' in which you describe the first holiday that you took with your family about which you have a clear memory. It could be a description of a visit to another country or simply an account of a day when you and your family went on a trip together.

Your account should focus on your memories of what happened and what you and other members of your family did.

Plan your work in the space below and then write your answer on separate paper.

_____

_____

_____

_____

_____

_____

_____

_____

_____

_____

Exercises

Punctuation: full stops and capital letters

Punctuate these sentences correctly by adding full stops and capital letters as appropriate.

1   we spent our holiday on a campsite in france it was very crowded

_____

_____

2   we visited paris which was as beautiful as i'd expected it is also full of interesting museums

_____

_____

3   my mother enjoyed the experience of living in a tent she said that it was easier to keep tidy than our house

_____

_____

4   when we arrived at the campsite we hired a small citroën car so that we could explore the area

_____

_____

5   on most days the weather was very hot and sunny it rained on only one day

_____

_____

6   on most nights we ate in the campsite restaurant there was a good range of food to suit the tastes of the whole family

_____

_____

7 we also visited the house and gardens where the artist claude monet used to live there were very many other tourists there on the day we went

_____

_____

8 the french people that we met were all very friendly and appreciated our attempts to speak their language

_____

_____

9 the part of france we were in is called normandy i want to visit provence next year which is another part of the same country

_____

_____

10 it is said to be very beautiful and its beaches are on the shore of the mediterranean sea

_____

_____

If you have correctly identified all the beginnings and ends of sentences (as well as spotting the proper nouns), you should have: 17 sentences, 17 full stops and 29 capital letters.

Parts of speech: pronouns and possessive adjectives

In order to write English accurately, it is important to be in full control of pronouns and possessive adjectives. The table below lists pronouns and possessive adjectives for your reference. Remind yourself of these and then answer the questions that follow.

Personal pronouns		Possessive adjectives and pronouns		Reflexive pronouns
Subject form	Object form	Possessive adjective	Possessive pronoun	
I	me	my	mine	myself
you	you	your	yours	yourself
he	him	his	his	himself
she	her	her	hers	herself
it	it	its	its	itself
we	us	our	ours	ourselves
you	you	your	yours	yourselves
they	them	their	theirs	themselves

Complete these sentences by inserting the correct form of the personal pronoun or possessive adjective.

1 This house is _____ (*you*).

2 He gave the present to _____ (*I*).

3 Is this _____ (*they*) car?

4 Where is _____ (*you*) sister going tonight?

5 I know where Rohan and his family live. This house is _____ (*they*).

6 This is a photo of _____ (*I*) friend, Shivane.

7 _____ (*She*) family live in a large house.

8 She has a pet cat. The basket is _____ (*it*).

9 This house is _____ (*we*).

10 Rohan lives next door with _____ (*he*) mother, father and sister.

11 Who is _____ (*you*) best friend?

12 We visited _____ (*they*) during the summer holidays.

Parts of speech: prepositions

Another feature of the English language that it is important to be in control of is the correct use of prepositions. The next exercise will test your skills in this area.

Complete these sentences by choosing the correct preposition.

1 To reach the library you have to go _____ (*up/over*) these stairs and then _____ (*down/into*) a long corridor.

2 I watched a programme _____ (*for/about*) elephants _____ (*by/on*) the television.

3 He drove _____ (*over/towards*) me without slowing down, swerved at the last minute and then sped off _____ (*towards/at*) the town centre.

4 He drove _____ (*under/through*) the railway bridge and then _____ (*past/through*) the town hall.

5 She took the money _____ (*out of/into*) her bag and put it _____ (*into/at*) the safe.

6 I'll meet you _____ (*in/at/on*) 6 o'clock.

7 I've been waiting here _____ (*for/while/during*) 30 minutes.

8 Who is responsible _____ (*for/of/with*) this delay?

9 She went _____ (*to/at/on*) her friend's birthday party.

10 I'm not very keen _____ (*for/with/on*) the blue dress. I prefer the red one.

Teacher comments

Descriptive writing

Reading

The next two passages are examples of descriptive writing. Extract 1 is taken from the famous Sherlock Holmes mystery story *The Hound of the Baskervilles* and describes the interior of a rather gloomy house in a remote part of the English countryside. As you read it, you could consider how the description helps to set the scene for the mysterious events that follow later in the story.

Extract 2 is from the nineteenth-century novel *Vanity Fair* by W.M. Thackeray and introduces the comic (but also rather sad) character of Jos Sedley – a would-be fashionable young man who is both too old and too fat to be the type of character he would like to be!

Read Extract 1 carefully and then answer the questions that follow.

Extract 1: Baskerville Hall

A square balustraded gallery ran round the top of the old hall, approached by a double stair. From this central point two long corridors extended the whole length of the building, from which all the bedrooms opened. My own was in the same wing as Baskerville's and almost next door to it. These rooms appeared to be much more modern than the central part of the house, and the bright paper and numerous candles did something to remove the sombre impression which our arrival had left upon my mind.

But the dining room which opened out of the hall was a place of shadow and gloom. It was a long chamber with a step separating the dais where the family sat from the lower portion reserved for their dependants. At one end a minstrel's gallery overlooked it. Black beams shot across above our heads, with a smoke-darkened ceiling beyond them. With rows of flaring torches to light it up, and the colour and rude hilarity of an old-time banquet, it might have softened; but now, when two black-clothed gentlemen sat in the little circle of light thrown by a shaded lamp, one's voice became hushed and one's spirit subdued. A dim line of ancestors, in every variety of dress, from the Elizabethan knight to the buck [trendsetter] of the Regency, stared down upon us and daunted us by their silent company. We talked little, and I for one was glad when the meal was over and we were able to retire into the modern billiard room.

****

I drew aside my curtains before I went to bed and looked out from my window. It opened upon the grassy space which lay in front of the hall door. Beyond, two copses of trees moaned and swung in a rising wind. A half moon broke through the rifts of racing clouds. In its cold light I saw beyond the trees a broken fringe of rocks, and the long, low curve of the melancholy moor. I closed the curtain, feeling that my last impression was in keeping with the rest.

Sir Arthur Conan Doyle

Now answer these questions on Extract 1. You should try to use your own words in your answers as much as possible.

1 Explain the meaning of the following words and phrases as used in the passage:

a) balustraded _____

b) sombre _____

c) rude hilarity _____

d) daunted _____

e) melancholy _____

2 Explain, using your own words, the layout of the dining room. ('It was a long chamber … for their dependants.')

_____

_____

3 Describe the behaviour of the writer and his companions while they were in the dining room.

_____

4 Why do you think that the diners 'talked little'?

_____

_____

5 Explain as fully as you can what the writer means in the last sentence of the passage.

_____

_____

6 This passage comes from the early stages of a mystery story. Say at what period of history you think the story is set. Then by referring closely to the writer's language and choice of words explain how he creates an atmosphere of mystery and suspense.

_____

_____

_____

_____

_____

_____

_____

_____

_____

In the next passage Jos Sedley has recently returned to London after a period of working in India, where he contracted a liver disease. Some of the language is explained for you. George 'Beau' Brummell (1778–1840) was a leading fashion icon (a 'dandy') of the Regency Period in England and a friend of George IV.

Read Extract 2 carefully and then answer the questions that follow.

Extract 2: Jos Sedley

Luckily, at this time he caught a liver complaint, for the cure of which he returned to Europe, and which was the source of great comfort and amusement to him in his native country. He did not live with his family while in London, but had lodgings of his own, like a gay young bachelor. Before he went to India he was too young to partake of the delightful pleasures of a man about town, and plunged into them on his return with considerable assiduity. He drove his horses in the Park; he dined at the fashionable taverns (for the Oriental Club was not as yet invented); he frequented the theatres, as the mode was in those days, or made his appearance at the opera, laboriously attired in tights and a cocked hat.

On returning to India, and ever after, he used to talk of the pleasure of this period of his existence with great enthusiasm, and give you to understand that he and Brummell were the leading bucks [trendsetters] of the day. But he was as lonely here as in his jungle at Boggley Wollah. He scarcely knew a single soul in the metropolis: and were it not for his doctor, and the society of his blue-pill, and his liver complaint, he must have died of loneliness. He was lazy, peevish, and a *bon-vivant* [someone who lives well]; the appearance of a lady frightened him beyond measure; hence it was but seldom that he joined the paternal circle in Russell Square, where there was plenty of gaiety, and where the jokes of his good natured old father frightened his *amour-propre* [self-esteem]. His bulk caused Joseph much anxious thought and alarm; now and then he would make a desperate attempt to get rid of his superabundant fat; but his indolence and love of good living speedily got the better of these endeavours at reform, and he found himself again at his three meals a day. He never was well dressed; but he took the hugest pains to adorn his big person, and passed many hours daily in that occupation. His valet [servant] made a fortune out of his wardrobe [collection of clothes]: his toilet-table was covered with as many pomatums [dressings for the hair] and essences as ever were employed by an old beauty: he had tried, in order to give himself a waist, every girth, stay, and waistband then invented. Like most fat men, he *would* have his clothes made too tight, and took care they should be of the most brilliant colours and youthful cut. When dressed at length, in the afternoon, he would issue forth to take a drive with nobody in the Park; and then would come back in order to dress again and go and dine with nobody at the Piazza Coffee-House. He was as vain as a girl; and perhaps his extreme shyness was one of the results of his extreme vanity.

W.M. Thackeray

Now answer these questions. You should try to use your own words in your answers as much as possible.

1   Explain the meaning of the following words and phrases as used in the passage:

   a) to partake of _____

   b) assiduity _____

   c) as the mode was in those days _____

   d) metropolis _____

   e) peevish _____

   f) superabundant _____

   g) indolence _____

   h) endeavours at reform _____

2   What does the word 'laboriously' in line 10 suggest about Jos's way of dressing?

   _____

   _____

3 Do you think that Jos really was as well known in London society as Beau Brummell? You should quote from the passage to support your answer.

_____

4 Why was Jos unwilling to mix in his father's social circle?

_____

5 How do you think that Jos's valet was able to make a fortune out of his wardrobe?

_____

_____

6 Using your own words, make a list of the main features of Jos's character and appearance that are mentioned in the passage.

_____

_____

_____

7 What do you think is the writer's true opinion of Jos Sedley? Does he think he is a fool? Is he laughing at him? Does he show any sympathy towards him? Explain your comments as fully as you can and refer closely to the passage in your answer.

_____

_____

_____

_____

_____

_____

_____

_____

_____

Writing task

Write a description of your favourite local shop and of some of the people who work in it. Try to capture the sights, sounds and overall atmosphere of the place.

Plan your work in the space below and then write your answer on separate paper.

_____

_____

_____

_____

_____

_____

_____

_____

_____

_____

_____

_____

Exercise

Punctuation: commas

Rewrite these sentences, inserting commas where necessary.

1 Mrs Singh the Headteacher is a very caring person.

_____

2 On the bedroom shelf were books an alarm clock some toys and a glass containing water.

_____

_____

3 The group's first album in my opinion is the best they ever made.

_____

_____

4 That was an enjoyable meal don't you agree?

_____

5 Because of their strange and unnatural appearance clowns may terrify some children.

_____

_____

6 Excuse me sir can you direct me to the library?

_____

7 Her birthday the last day in March was a very special celebration.

_____

_____

8 Having set off much too quickly Lee finished last in the 1500 metres race.

_____

_____

9 Slowly clumsily and making far too much noise Ravi failed to leave the house without anyone knowing.

_____

_____

10 I'm sorry but no I'm sure I was told to expect you for lunch today.

_____

_____

Teacher comments

Non-fiction

Reading

The three passages that follow are all examples of non-fiction writing in which the writers are concerned with giving true rather than imagined accounts. The first passage outlines the main details of the life of the author Roald Dahl, while the second and third passages both describe the French town of Boulogne-sur-Mer. Although all of these examples consist mainly of factual details, when reading them you should also think about how much the personal opinions of the writers make themselves known.

First read carefully the passage below about Roald Dahl and answer the questions that follow.

Roald Dahl

Roald Dahl's parents were from Norway, but he was born in Wales on 13 September 1916. The family used to spend the summer holidays on a little Norwegian island, swimming, fishing and going by boat. When Roald was four years old, his father died, so his mother had to organise the trip alone for herself and her six children.

After school, Roald Dahl didn't go to university, but applied for a job at the Shell Company, because he was sure they would send him abroad. He was sent to East Africa, where he got the adventure he wanted: great heat, crocodiles, snakes and safaris. He lived in the jungle, learned to speak Swahili and suffered from malaria. When the Second World War broke out, he went to Nairobi to join the Royal Air Force. He was a fighter pilot and shot down German planes but got shot down himself. After six months in hospital he flew again.

In 1942, he went to Washington as Assistant Air Attaché [a post in the British Embassy]. There, he started writing short stories. His collections of short stories have been translated into many languages and have been best-sellers all over the world. He wrote TV series like *Tales of the Unexpected* and the novel *My Uncle Oswald*.

His books are mostly fantasy, and full of imagination. They are always a little cruel, but never without humour – a thrilling mixture of the grotesque and comic.

Roald Dahl didn't only write books for grown-ups, but also for children, such as *James and the Giant Peach*, *Fantastic Mr Fox* and *The Gremlins*. About his children's stories he said once: 'I make my points by exaggerating wildly. That's the only way to get through to children.' Roald Dahl is perhaps the most popular and best-selling children's book author. However, these stories are so sarcastic and humorous that adults also appreciate reading them.

Roald Dahl died on 23 November 1990. *The Times* newspaper called him 'one of the most widely read and influential writers of our generation'.

Now answer these questions. You should try to use your own words in your answers as much as possible.

1 Explain the meaning of the following words and phrases as used in the passage:

    a) fantasy _____

    b) a thrilling mixture of the grotesque and comic _____

    _____

    c) exaggerating wildly _____

    d) influential _____

2 What did Roald Dahl do after he left school and why?

_____

3 From the information given in paragraph 2, what conclusions can you make about Roald Dahl's character and interests?

_____

_____

4 What do you think makes Roald Dahl's books for adults particularly appealing to readers? (You should refer to the passage in your answer.)

_____

_____

5 What was Roald Dahl's trick for making his stories interesting for young readers?

_____

_____

6 Why, according to the writer, are Roald Dahl's books for children enjoyed by adults as well?

_____

_____

7 This is a non-fiction piece of writing; however, it is not entirely factual. Write down all the opinions that it contains.

_____

_____

_____

Read carefully both the following passages about Boulogne-sur-Mer and answer the questions that follow them.

The first description is taken from a modern-day guide to the town and the second is an account of a visit made by a Scottish writer, Tobias Smollett, in 1763.

Boulogne-sur-Mer – Description 1

The Old Walled Town

After watching the boats and the fishermen for a while, take a walk from the quayside car park, through the centre of Boulogne-sur-Mer and up the hill to the Old Town, contained within its magnificent walls. Just head away from the port area and keep walking up the hill towards the Basilica [cathedral] which stands on the hilltop in the middle of the Old Town. You will most likely arrive at the principal gate to the walled area, the Porte des Dunes.

While walking up to the Old Town, you will pass through the town centre with its bustling selection of shops, brasseries and cafés. The Church of St Nicolas, protector of sailors, dominates the cobbled square in the town centre where the market is held on Saturday mornings.

Like all local markets in France it is full of fresh, local produce.
The Old Town has four gates: Porte des Dunes (West), Porte Neuve
(North), Porte Gayole (East) and Porte des Degres (South). The main
entrance, which you will probably arrive at if you have walked up
from the town centre, is Porte des Dunes, next to the little Tourist
Information Cabin. Once through the gate, within the walls there is a
network of little streets, with their very well preserved stone buildings.

The thirteenth-century castle houses the Château-Musée de Boulogne-
sur-Mer – an important art museum with a collection of Greek
ceramics, European fine arts and Egyptian antiques. Other important
buildings are the Hôtel de Ville [town hall], the Palais de Justice,
Napoleon's Palace and of course the Basilica, with its magnificent dome
which is the second largest in Europe. The dome of St Peter's in Rome is
the only one that is bigger. The narrow road from the square up to the
Basilica (Rue de Lille) is very enticing with all its little restaurants with
their tables and chairs spilling out onto the pavement.

Boulogne-sur-Mer – Description 2

Boulogne is divided into the Upper and Lower Towns. The former is a kind
of citadel, about a short mile in circumference, situated on a rising ground,
surrounded by a high wall and rampart, planted with rows of trees, which
form a delightful walk. It commands a fine view of the country and Lower
Town; and in clear weather the coast of England, from Dover to Folkstone,
appears so plain, that one would imagine it was within four or five leagues
[12 or 15 miles or about 20 km] of the French shore. The Upper Town was
formerly fortified with outworks, which are now in ruins. Here is a square,
a town-house, the cathedral, and two or three convents of nuns; in one of
which there are several English girls, sent hither for their education.

The Lower Town is continued from the gate of the Upper Town, down the
slope of a hill, as far as the harbour, stretching on both sides to a large
extent, and is much more considerable than the Upper, with respect to the
beauty of the streets, the convenience of the houses, and the number and
wealth of the inhabitants. These, however, are all merchants, or bourgeoise
[middle classes], for the noblesse or gentry live all together in the Upper

Town, and never mix with the others. The harbour of Boulogne is at the mouth of the small river, or rather rivulet Liane, which is so shallow, that the children wade through it at low water. As the tide makes, the sea flows in, and forms a pretty extensive harbour, which, however, admits nothing but small vessels. It is contracted at the mouth by two stone jetties or piers, which seem to have been constructed by some engineer very little acquainted with this branch of his profession; for they are carried out in such a manner as to collect a bank of sand just at the entrance of the harbour. The road is very open and unsafe, and the surf very high when the wind blows from the sea.

Tobias Smollett

Now answer the following questions on these two descriptions of Boulogne-sur-Mer. You should try to use your own words in your answers as much as possible.

1 Explain the meaning of the following words and phrases as used in the first description of Boulogne-sur-Mer.

    a) principal _____

    b) very well preserved _____

    c) ceramics _____

    d) enticing _____

2 Explain the meaning of the following words and phrases as used in the second description of the town.

    a) rampart _____

    b) as the tide makes _____

    c) pretty extensive _____

    d) contracted _____

Extended task

Write a detailed comparison of the similarities and differences between these two descriptions of Boulogne-sur-Mer. Plan your answer carefully by making notes in the table below. You should consider the following points in particular:

- details mentioned in both passages
- details mentioned in only one of the passages
- the attitude of the writers towards the details they mention
- the **facts** mentioned by each writer
- the **opinions** given by each writer
- the audience for whom you think each passage was written
- any points that link the passages to the specific historic period in which they were written.

When you have completed your notes, write them up as a piece of continuous prose of three or four paragraphs on a separate sheet of paper.

Description 1	Description 2

Writing task

You recently left an item (e.g. a book, musical instrument, piece of sports equipment) on the bus on your way home from school. Write two letters:

a) a formal letter to the bus company describing the item, giving details of when and where it was lost and asking for information about where to collect it if it has been found

b) a letter to your cousin who lives in a different town describing what happened after you discovered that you had lost the item.

Make sure that you include all necessary addresses, and so on, and that the greeting and ending of each letter is appropriate for the person to whom it will be sent.

Plan your work in the space below and then write your letters on separate paper.

_____

_____

_____

_____

_____

_____

Exercises

Punctuation: apostrophes

In each question, only one of the sentences has all the apostrophes placed correctly. Tick (✔) the box next to the correct sentence.

1 **a)** The town's shopping mall is one of the countrys busiest. ☐

b) The towns shopping mall is one of the country's busiest. ☐

c) The town's shopping mall is one of the country's busiest. ☐

d) The towns' shopping mall is one of the countrys' busiest. ☐

2 a) The two girl's calculators were left in the school's canteen. ☐

b) The two girls calculator's were left in the schools' canteen. ☐

c) The two girls' calculators were left in the school's canteen. ☐

d) The two girls' calculators' were left in the schools canteen. ☐

3 a) My parent's house is in one of the city's quietest areas. ☐

b) My parents' house is in one of the citys quietest areas. ☐

c) My parents' house is in one of the citys' quietest areas. ☐

d) My parents' house is in one of the city's quietest areas. ☐

4 a) The film's audiences were quick to praise the two actors' skill. ☐

b) The film's audiences were quick to praise the two actor's skill. ☐

c) The films audiences were quick to praise the two actors' skill. ☐

d) The films' audiences were quick to praise the two actors' skill. ☐

5 a) Rohan's fathers office is very close to his only uncle's shop. ☐

b) Rohans father's office is very close to his only uncle's shop. ☐

c) Rohan's fathers' office is very close to his only uncles' shop. ☐

d) Rohan's father's office is very close to his only uncle's shop. ☐

CHAPTER 4

6 **a)** The two cars wheels' hubs' were damaged in the collision. ☐

  b) The two cars wheels hub's were damaged in the collision. ☐

  c) The two cars' wheels' hubs were damaged in the collision. ☐

  d) The two car's wheel's hubs were damaged in the collision. ☐

7 **a)** The band's noise levels were giving its audience headaches. ☐

  b) The band's noise levels were giving it's audience headaches. ☐

  c) The bands' noise levels were giving its audience headaches. ☐

  d) The bands' noise levels' were giving its audience headaches. ☐

8 **a)** The teams striker's attitude was affecting all the player's confidence. ☐

  b) The team's striker's attitude was affecting all the players' confidence. ☐

  c) The teams striker's attitude was affecting all the players' confidence. ☐

  d) The team's striker's attitude was affecting all the player's confidence. ☐

9 **a)** It's teachers made the school's reputation very high. ☐

  b) Its teachers made the school's reputation very high. ☐

  c) Its teachers' made the schools' reputation very high. ☐

  d) It's teachers made the schools' reputation very high. ☐

10 a) The teacher's knowledge made him all the students' favourite. ☐

  b) The teachers' knowledge made him all the students' favourite. ☐

  c) The teachers' knowledge made him all the student's favourite. ☐

  d) The teachers knowledge made him all the students favourite. ☐

Choosing the right word

Read the descriptive passage below carefully and try to build up a clear picture in your mind of the scene being described.

Write out the passage choosing the best words from the options given. There are no absolutely correct answers – the important thing is that you consider the choices carefully in order to produce a consistent and convincing description.

The sky (*frowned/glared/sulked*) over the town. In the streets pedestrians (*quaking/shaking/shivering*) in the wind and driving rain (*dragged/stumbled/trudged*) past shops. Cars (*crawled/dawdled/plodded*) along the road, their drivers (*blinking/squinting/staring*) as their windscreen wipers (*clunked/knocked/thudded*) monotonously. It had been raining (*ceaselessly/consistently/solidly*) for three hours and the water (*gurgled/splashed/spluttered*) as it (*flowed/ran/streamed*) from the gutters onto the (*overflowing/teeming/gushing*) sidewalk. The only relief from the (*deluge/downpour/storm*) could be found within the Percolator Coffee House, whose (*civil/sympathetic/welcoming*) interior offered (*animation/solace/warmth*) and comfort.

_____

_____

_____

_____

_____

_____

_____

_____

_____

Writing formal letters

Lee was not happy with an electrical item that he bought and has written a letter of complaint to the store from which he purchased it. Unfortunately, not only did a gremlin get into his computer and jumble up his letter but he has also written the letter using an inappropriate tone and has failed to give precise information.

Unscramble and rewrite the letter, making sure that it is written in a suitable tone and contains all the necessary information. (You can make up names and addresses.)

As soon as I tried to turn it on there was a spark and a flash and the screen went blank.

You had better replace this straight away or else I will send my big brother and his friends round to sort you out.

53 Riverside Road Blanktown BT3 1XX Thursday

Sometime last week I bought a Vistascreen Game Player from one of your stores.

Cheers, Lee

I want to make a complaint about an item you sold me.

The Boss HappyKid Game Shops Blanktown

I want you to tell me what you are going to do about this.

Dear Person in Charge

_____

_____

_____

_____

_____

_____

_____

_____

_____

_____

_____

_____

_____

_____

_____

_____

_____

_____

Teacher comments

5 Folk tales

Reading

A fable is a type of folk tale that contains a moral or a lesson for the reader. Here is a fable by the Greek storyteller Aesop, who lived about 2500 years ago. The moral still holds true today.

Read the fable carefully and then answer the questions that follow.

Extract 1: 'The Man, the Boy and the Donkey'

A man and his son were once going with their donkey to market. As they were walking along by its side a countryman passed them and said: 'You fools, what is a donkey for but to ride upon?'

So the man put the boy on the donkey and they went on their way. But soon they passed a group of men, one of whom said: 'See that lazy youngster, he lets his father walk while he rides.'

So the man ordered his boy to get off, and got on himself. But they hadn't gone far when they passed two women, one of whom said to the other: 'Shame on that lazy lout to let his poor little son trudge along.'

Well, the man didn't know what to do, but at last he took his boy up before him on the donkey. By this time they had come to the town, and the passers-by began to jeer and point at them. The man stopped and asked what they were scoffing at. The men said:

'Aren't you ashamed of yourself for overloading that poor donkey of yours with yourself and your hulking son?'

The man and boy got off and tried to think what to do. They thought and they thought, till at last they cut down a pole, tied the donkey's feet to it, and raised the pole and the donkey to their shoulders. They went along amid the laughter of all who met them till they came to Market Bridge, when the donkey, getting one of his feet loose, kicked out and caused the boy to drop his end of the pole. In the struggle the donkey fell over the bridge, and his fore-feet being tied together, he was drowned.

'That will teach you,' said an old man who had followed them.

Now answer these questions. You should try to use your own words in your answers as much as possible.

1   Explain the meaning of the following words and phrases as used in the passage:

   a) lout _____

   b) trudge along _____

   c) jeer _____

   d) scoffing at _____

   e) hulking _____

2   What was the countryman's reason for calling the father and son 'fools' in paragraph 1?

   _____

3   What was the point of the comment made by the group of men in paragraph 2?

   _____

   _____

4   Explain, using your own words, what the women's criticism of the father was.

   _____

   _____

5   What did the group of men in the town accuse the father and son of doing?

   _____

6 How did the man, the boy and the donkey finally arrive at Market Bridge and what happened after they reached there?

_____

_____

7 Explain, as fully as you can, what you think the moral of this story is.

_____

_____

The next story is a modern retelling of a folk tale from India. Read it carefully and then answer the questions that follow.

Extract 2: 'King of the Birds'

The birds of the jungle had no king. It was a real embarrassment for them since everyone else in the jungle had a king.

A king is someone who heads the flock and decides everything for them. All the birds decided they too needed a king. They called a meeting to resolve the problem.

But who would be the king?

The Mynah bird had an idea. 'Let the bird who can fly the highest be made king of the air,' she said.

One of the birds, Eagle, was a braggart. He was big and strong, and was sure that he would win.

He strutted around, and asked: 'Why not make me king now? You know I can fly the highest.'

'Still, you may not win,' piped a little voice. Eagle turned to see who had said that. It was Sparrow. 'Oh!' he said in a mocking voice. 'And who's going to beat me? You?' he asked, letting out a loud, crackling laugh.

The little birds, the middle-sized birds and the big birds all got ready for the race. It was decided that Owl should start the race. When everyone was ready, Owl cried, 'Whoo, whoo!'

As soon as Owl signalled, all the birds took to the air.

Up, up, up they went, far into the blue sky.

But they could not fly very high and very fast for long. One by one, they dropped out of the race. Only Eagle went on flying, as strong as ever. 'High, high … I'm a bird in the sky … I'm an eagle that flies so high,' he sang. At length, he looked below him and saw that all the birds had given up.

'Oh! What did I say!' he exclaimed. 'I am king of the air and all the birds that fly.'

What Eagle did not know was that tiny Sparrow had been flying under his wing. The moment he stopped, Sparrow darted out. He flew just above Eagle's head and cried out, 'No, no, no, Mr Eagle. I'm king of the birds. Look, I've flown higher than you.'

All the birds agreed with Sparrow. In any case, they were glad to see proud Eagle beaten. He had boasted too much. So they chose Sparrow as their king.

Eagle did not like this at all. He could not bear to see the crown being placed on Sparrow's head. So he caught the little bird in his claws and threw him to the ground.

Although Sparrow did not get hurt, he found that Eagle had torn away half his tail. 'Oh well! I'll still be king,' he told himself.

And ever since, Sparrow has had a short tail.

Brishti Bandyopadhyay

Now answer these questions. You should try to use your own words in your answers as much as possible.

1   Explain the meaning of the following words and phrases as used in the passage:

   a) real embarrassment _____

   b) resolve the problem _____

   c) braggart _____

   d) strutted _____

e) mocking _____

f) exclaimed _____

2 Give **two** reasons, taken from the passage, why the birds wanted to have a king.

_____

_____

_____

3 The words 'piped' and 'loud, crackling' are used in the story to describe sounds the birds make. How do these words help you to understand the characters of Sparrow and Eagle?

_____

_____

_____

4 Explain fully, using your own words, how Sparrow managed to fly higher than Eagle.

_____

_____

5 Why do you think that the other birds agreed that Sparrow should be their king?

_____

6 By referring closely to the passage, list as many differences as you can between Sparrow and Eagle.

_____

_____

_____

7 Explain as fully as you can what you think the moral is of this story. (You may consider that there is more than one moral; if so, explain them all.)

_____

_____

_____

_____

Writing task

Research either in a library or on the internet into traditional folk tales or fables. When you have found one whose moral appeals to you, write your own updated version of the story, setting it within the world with which you are familiar.

Plan your work in the space below and then write your story on separate paper.

_____

_____

_____

_____

_____

_____

_____

_____

_____

_____

_____

_____

Exercises

Punctuation: apostrophes

1   Rewrite these sentences so that the words underlined are in the possessive form. Use apostrophes where necessary.

a) The best friend of her <u>sister</u> is a nurse.

_____

b) We saw the ball of the <u>children</u> in the middle of the garden.

_____

c) The teachers of the <u>twins</u> could not tell them apart.

_____

d) The conclusion, drawn by the two <u>scientists,</u> could not be questioned.

_____

e) The excitement of the <u>play</u> increased in the second act.

_____

f) I'm sure the solution of <u>anybody</u> is better than mine.

_____

g) When I was a child I spent all of my holidays at the farm of my <u>grandparents</u>.

_____

h) The votes of three <u>teachers</u> decided who won the prize.

_____

i) The front wheel of your <u>bicycle</u> has a puncture.

_____

j) The dog chased the ball that belonged to <u>it</u>.

_____

2 Rewrite the following sentences with the words in brackets written in their contracted form. Make sure you choose the right spelling for each contraction. Remember that the apostrophe takes the place of the missing letter or letters.

a) I (did not) eat my supper yesterday.

_____

b) (You are) being very foolish.

_____

c) (He would) often arrive late for school.

_____

d) (She is) the best behaved student in the class.

_____

e) We (can not) be late for the party tonight.

_____

f) I (had not) finished my homework when my friend arrived.

_____

g) (We have) never been on holiday to Australia.

_____

h) (I will) make sure that I remember your birthday.

_____

i) You (will not) forget that tomorrow is my birthday.

_____

j) Surely she (would not) forget to buy me a present.

_____

Punctuation: direct speech

Here are the opening paragraphs of a short story entitled 'The Tidy Drawer'. However, all full stops, commas, speech marks and capital letters (apart from those for characters' names) have been left out. Rewrite the passage with the correct punctuation, including paragraphs. You will need to put in some question marks.

one saturday morning Abby's mum came upstairs to see Abby in her bedroom or tried to there was so much mess on the floor she could only poke her head around the door Abby sat in the middle of it all reading a book

What a tip Mum said you need to have a clear up in here why Abby asked why Mum repeated because things get broken or lost when they're all willy-nilly like this come on have a tidy up now but I'm very busy Abby argued and it's boring on my own can't you help me no I can't I'm busy too but I'll give you extra pocket money if you do a good job

When Mum came back later all the toys and clothes and books had disappeared i'm impressed said Mum but I'll inspect it properly later it was easy said Abby can I have my extra pocket money now all right get it out of my change purse it's in the kitchen tidy drawer

In the kitchen Abby went over to the dresser and pulled open the tidy drawer she hunted for the purse any luck Mum asked Abby shook her head it must be lurking at the bottom Mum said let's have a proper look

_____

_____

_____

_____

_____

_____

_____

_____

_____

_____

_____

_____

_____

_____

_____

_____

_____

Teacher comments

Reading

This chapter looks at a complete contemporary short story by the American writer Mike Krath. The story is divided into two parts with questions following each part. These questions will test your understanding of what happens in the story and also help you to consider the techniques used by the storyteller.

Chapter 7 looks at another short story: a traditional ghost story from the Ukraine. At the end of this second story, you will find a question that asks you to write about both these stories in greater detail (see page 74).

Here is the first part of Mike Krath's story. Read it carefully and then answer the questions that follow this first part.

'High and Lifted Up' – Part 1

It was a windy day.

The mailman barely made it to the front door. When the door opened, Mrs Pennington said, 'Hello', but, before she had a real chance to say 'thank you', the mail blew out of the mailman's hands, into the house, and the front door slammed in his face. Mrs Pennington ran to pick up the mail.

'Oh my,' she said.

Tommy was watching the shutters open and then shut, open and then shut.

'Mom,' he said, 'may I go outside?'

'Be careful,' she said. 'It's so windy today.'

Tommy crawled down from the window-seat and ran to the door. He opened it with a bang. The wind blew fiercely and snatched the newly recovered mail from Mrs Pennington's hands and blew it even further into the house.

'Oh my,' she said again. Tommy ran outside and the door slammed shut.

Outside, yellow, gold, and red leaves were leaping from swaying trees, landing on the roof, jumping off the roof, and then chasing one another down the street in tiny whirlwinds of merriment.

Tommy watched in fascination.

'If I was a leaf, I would fly clear across the world,' Tommy thought and then ran out into the yard among the swirl of colours.

Mrs Pennington came to the front porch.

'Tommy, I have your jacket. Please put it on.'

However, there was no Tommy in the front yard.

'Tommy?'

Tommy was a leaf. He was blowing down the street with the rest of his playmates.

A maple leaf came close by, touched him and moved ahead. Tommy met him shortly, brushed against him, and moved further ahead. They swirled around and around, hit cars and poles, flew up into the air and then down again.

'This is fun,' Tommy thought.

Mike Krath

Now answer these questions. You should try to use your own words in your answers as much as possible.

1   Explain the meaning of the following words and phrases as used in the passage:

   a) the newly recovered mail _____

   _____

   b) tiny whirlwinds of merriment _____

   c) watched in fascination _____

   d) swirl of colours _____

2   Why did the mailman only 'barely' make it to the front door?

_____

3   Explain fully what happens to the mail up until the point where Tommy leaves the house.

_____

_____

_____

4   Note down the verbs used by the writer in the paragraph beginning 'Outside, yellow, gold …' and comment on how the choice of these words helps to bring the scene alive.

_____

_____

_____

5   Explain what you think Tommy was feeling when he was outside in the yard. You should refer to the passage to support your answer.

_____

_____

_____

6   Why was Mrs Pennington unable to find Tommy when she came out of the house with his jacket?

_____

7   What have you learnt about Mrs Pennington from this section of the story?

_____

_____

_____

Next read carefully the second part of the story and then answer the questions that follow.

'High and Lifted Up' – Part 2

The maple leaf blew in front of him. It was bright red with well defined veins. The sunlight shone through it giving it a brilliance never before seen by a little boy's eyes.

'Where do you think we are going?' Tommy asked the leaf.

'Does it matter?' the leaf replied. 'Have fun. Life is short.'

'I beg to differ,' an older leaf said suddenly coming beside them. 'The journey may be short, but the end is the beginning.'

Tommy pondered this, the best a leaf could ponder.

'Where do we end up?'

'If the wind blows you in that direction,' the old leaf said, 'you will end up in the city dump.'

'I don't want that,' Tommy said.

'If you are blown in that direction, you will fly high into the air and see things that no leaf has seen before.'

'Follow me to the city dump,' the maple leaf said. 'Most of my friends are there.'

The wind blew Tommy and the maple leaf along. Tommy thought of his choices. He wanted to continue to play.

'Okay,' Tommy said, 'I will go with you to the dump.'

The winds shifted and Tommy and the leaf were blown in the direction of the city dump.

The old leaf didn't follow. He was blown further down the block and suddenly lifted up high into the air.

'Hey,' he called out, 'the sights up here. They are spectacular. Come and see.'

Tommy and the maple leaf ignored him.

'I see something. I see the dump,' the old leaf cried out. 'I see smoke. Come up here. I see fire.'

'I see nothing,' the maple leaf said.

Tommy saw the fence that surrounded the city dump. He was happy to be with his friend. They would have fun in the dump.

Suddenly, a car pulled up. It was Tommy's mom. Mrs Pennington wasn't about to let her little boy run into the city dump.

'Not so fast,' she said getting out of the car. 'You are not allowed to play in there. Don't you see the smoke?'

Tommy watched the maple leaf blow against the wall and struggle to get over. He ran over to get it but was unable to reach it.

Mrs Pennington walked over and took the leaf. She put it in her pocket.

'There,' she said, 'it will be safe until we get home.'

Tommy smiled, ran to the car and got in. He rolled down the back window and looked up into the sky. He wondered where the old leaf had gone. Perhaps one day he would see what the old leaf had seen – perhaps.

Mike Krath

Now answer these questions. You should try to use your own words in your answers as much as possible.

1   Explain the meaning of the following words and phrases as used in the passage:

  a) well defined veins _____

  b) brilliance _____

  c) ponder _____

  d) spectacular _____

  e) ignored _____

2   Explain as fully as you can what the old leaf means by 'The journey may be short, but the end is the beginning.'

_____

_____

3 How does the old leaf's point of view differ from that of the maple leaf?

_____

_____

4 Why does Tommy agree to follow the maple leaf to the city dump?

_____

5 Why do you think Tommy should have listened to the old leaf and not ignored him?

_____

_____

6 Looking back at the story as a whole, do you think Tommy really turned into a leaf? Give reasons for your answer.

_____

_____

7 What point do you think the writer is making by presenting Tommy with the views of the old leaf and the maple leaf? What do you think Tommy has learnt by the end of the story? Try to explain your response to the story as fully as you can.

_____

_____

_____

_____

_____

If you have already read and answered the questions on the ghost story 'Cow's Head' in Chapter 7, you could now try the extended task on page 74, which asks you to compare this story with 'High and Lifted Up'.

Writing task

Imagine that you are the old leaf. Write the story of your life and recount some of the experiences that you have had. You should include the meeting with Tommy and the maple leaf and explain your thoughts about this event and these individuals.

Plan your work in the space below and then write your story on separate paper.

_____

_____

_____

_____

_____

_____

_____

_____

_____

_____

_____

_____

_____

_____

_____

_____

_____

Exercises

Punctuation: direct speech

When you use speech marks you need to remember the rule – **new speaker, new line**.

Rewrite the passage below, adding speech marks in the correct places. It is quite tricky. You will probably need to read through the passage several times to work out what each character is saying.

> Excuse me, said the stranger. Can you tell me where the library is?
> I'm not entirely sure because I'm a visitor here myself replied Anna.
> However, I went there with my friend a few days ago and I think it's very
> near the police station. The police station! said the stranger. That's good;
> I need to go there as well. Can you tell me how I get there from here?
> I think so said Anna. It's in the road after the railway station. You turn left
> at the next junction and then it's on your left. Thanks said the stranger,
> but which place will I be at then? Oh, sorry said Anna. That's the railway
> station. Go past there, cross the road and turn right and the police station
> is opposite you. I'm sure the library is a bit further down the same road.
> Thanks a lot said the man. You've been very helpful.

Punctuation: commas

The passage below is taken from Charles Dickens's novel *A Christmas Carol*.
It describes Ebenezer Scrooge, a miserable old miser. The passage is exactly as it was
originally written except that all the commas have been removed.

Write out the passage, adding the commas. The number missing is given for each
paragraph.

Oh! But he was a tight-fisted hand at the grindstone Scrooge! A squeezing
wrenching grasping scraping clutching covetous old sinner! Hard and
sharp as flint from which no steel had ever struck out generous fire; secret
and self-contained and solitary as an oyster. The cold within him froze his
old features nipped his pointed nose shrivelled his cheek stiffened his gait;
made his eyes red his thin lips blue; and spoke out shrewdly in his grating
voice. A frosty rime was on his head and on his eyebrows and his wiry
chin. He carried his own low temperature always about with him; he iced
his office in the dog-days; and didn't thaw it one degree at Christmas. (16)

External heat and cold had little influence on Scrooge. No warmth
could warm no wintry weather chill him. No wind that blew was
bitterer than he no falling snow was more intent upon its purpose no
pelting rain less open to entreaty. Foul weather didn't know where to
have him. The heaviest rain and snow and hail and sleet could boast
of the advantage over him in only one respect. They often came down
handsomely and Scrooge never did. (8)

_____

_____

_____

_____

_____

_____

_____

_____

Punctuation and paragraphs

Rewrite this passage, punctuating it by adding commas and full stops. You should also divide it into bullet-pointed paragraphs.

Build a House from Recycled Products
you may be surprised but it is possible to build a house using almost all recycled or recyclable material below are some examples of materials that can be used when building a house tyres can be packed with earth and arranged on top of one another like bricks and used as interior walls they can then be covered with plaster to absorb heat and provide insulation for the house this method reduces the amount of timber required in the building cellulose insulation material can be made from recycled newspapers and can provide insulation for the building recycled/recyclable steel can be used for many frameworks in a building steel can also be used for creating the roof plastic bottles can be recycled to make carpet material for the building and carpet pads can be made from reused textile recycled wood can be used for much of the interior of the house such as worktops cabinets and drawers reclaimed paint can be used to decorate the building once it has been fully built

_____

_____

_____

_____

_____

_____

_____

_____

_____

_____

_____

_____

_____

Teacher comments

Reading

This chapter is based on a retelling of a traditional ghost story from the Ukraine. The story has been divided into two parts with questions at the end of each part.

Read carefully the first part of the story and then answer the questions that follow. Try not to read to the end of the story before you have answered the questions on Part 1.

'Cow's Head' – Part 1

Oksana lived in a small house on the edge of town with her father, her stepmother and her stepsister. Oksana's stepmother disliked Oksana, favouring her true daughter, Olena.

Soon after her father's remarriage, Oksana found that all the housework fell to her while Olena idled her days away. Oksana's father was a timid man, and could not bring himself to defy his wife. So Oksana wore Olena's cast-off clothes, and her hands grew red and chapped from scrubbing in the cold, while Olena attended parties, growing lazy and spoiled.

One year, when the winter snows were particularly fierce, Oksana's family ran out of money. Oksana's stepmother began nagging her father to send Oksana away, because they could not afford to keep two girls. Reluctantly, Oksana's father agreed. He took Oksana to a cottage deep in the woods and left her there.

Oksana was very frightened. The woods were said to be filled with demons and monsters. But Oksana was also practical. She entered the cottage with her small bundle and found a fireplace, a lopsided table and a rusty old pot. Oksana put away the loaf of bread, the knife and the slab of cheese her father had given her. She folded the blanket and laid it near the fireplace. Then she collected wood and built a fire.

Oksana knew the bread and cheese would not last her all winter. So she made a snare using the thin, flexible branches of the trees and caught a snow rabbit to eat. She also dug under the deep snow, and found some roots and berries for food.

By dark, Oksana had melted snow for drinking water, and used the rest to make a stew. So Oksana ate well. Then she lay down near the fire for the night, listening to the wind howl and pretending to herself that she was not frightened of the woods.

Retold by S.E. Schlosser

Now answer these questions. You should try to use your own words in your answers as much as possible.

1 Explain the meaning of the following words and phrases as used in the passage:

   a) favouring _____

   b) idled her days away _____

   c) chapped _____

   d) reluctantly _____

   e) timid _____

   f) lopsided _____

2 Explain the relationships between Oksana and Olena and Oksana's father and his new wife.

   _____

   _____

   _____

   _____

3 State one household chore that was done by Oksana. _____

4 What is meant by 'Oksana was also practical' and how did Oksana show this when she was in the cottage in the woods?

_____

_____

_____

5 How did Oksana feed herself while she was in the woods?

_____

_____

_____

6 What was Oksana frightened of and how did she try to overcome this?

_____

_____

_____

7 **Before** you read Part 2 of the story, using clues from the passage, write down two or three events that you think will happen next in the story.

_____

_____

_____

Read carefully the second part of the story and then answer the questions that follow.

'Cow's Head' – Part 2

It was midnight when the knock came.

Knock, knock, knock.

It echoed hollowly through the dark cottage. Oksana woke with a start, her heart pounding in fear. It came again.

Knock, knock, knock.

Oksana thought of the monsters. She hid under her blanket, praying the thing would go away.

Knock, knock, knock.

Oksana rose, grabbing a branch. She crept towards the door. The wind howled eerily down the chimney. Oksana swallowed and swung the door open. There was nothing there. Her heart pounded fiercely as she stared out at the snow whipping about in the light of her small fire. Then she looked down. Oksana let out a shriek of terror and leapt back, dropping her stick. It was a demon. An evil spirit.

It had no body!

'Who are you?' Oksana stuttered, clutching the door with shaking hands.

'I am Cow's Head,' it replied.

Indeed, Oksana saw at once that it was. The head was brown, with curved horns and strange, haunted eyes.

'I am cold and hungry. May I sleep by your fire?' Cow's Head asked. Its voice was cold and lifeless.

Oksana gulped down her horror.

'Of course,' she said.

'Lift me over the threshold,' demanded Cow's Head hollowly. Oksana did as she was bidden.

'Place me near the fire.'

Anger warred with compassion inside her, but compassion won. Oksana put it next to the fire.

'I am hungry,' said Cow's Head. 'Feed me.'

Oksana thought of her meagre food supply. The stew left in the pot was for her breakfast. She fed it to Cow's Head.

'I will sleep now,' it said. There was no softening in its attitude toward her. Nonetheless, Oksana made it comfortable for the night, giving it her blanket and sleeping in a cold corner with only her cloak to keep her warm.

When she woke in the morning, Cow's Head was gone. Where it had slept was a large trunk, filled with the most beautiful gowns she had ever seen. Under the gowns lay heaps of gold and jewels.

Oksana stared blankly at the riches in front of her. Her father's voice roused her.

'Daughter, I am come.'

Oksana forgot the trunk in her joy. She ran into his arms. He had defied her stepmother to come and bring her back to their home.

'Papa, come see!' Oksana exclaimed as she pulled him into the cottage. Her words tumbled over each other as she explained.

Her father took her home. She was honoured in her town for her compassion and her bravery, and won scores of suitors. She married soon after her return from the cottage.

Hearing Oksana's story, and seeing the riches she had received, Olena went to the cottage in the forest and spent the night there. But when Cow's Head appeared, she was too lazy to serve it. In the morning, all her gowns had turned to rags and her possessions to dust.

But Oksana lived to a ripe old age in happiness and prosperity.

Retold by S.E. Schlosser

Now answer these questions. You should try to use your own words in your answers as much as possible.

1 Explain the meaning of the following words and phrases as used in the passage:

a) hollowly _____

b) eerily _____

c) the snow whipping about in the light of her small fire _____

_____

d) gulped down her horror _____

_____

e) did as she was bidden _____

f) compassion _____

g) prosperity _____

2 At the beginning of Part 2 of the story, there are several one-line paragraphs. What effect does the writer gain by using these?

_____

_____

3 From the paragraph beginning 'Oksana rose, grabbing a branch ...', give two statements that tell you that she was very scared.

_____

_____

4 What impression do the words 'cold and lifeless' and 'hollowly' give you of Cow's Head and the way in which it talks?

_____

_____

_____

5 What does the sentence 'Anger warred with compassion inside her, but compassion won.' tell you about Oksana's state of mind?

_____

_____

6 Which word tells you that Oksana had very little food to eat? _____

7 By referring closely to the conclusion of the story (from the paragraph beginning 'When she woke in the morning…' to the end) explain as fully as you can what has happened to Oksana, Olena and Oksana's father and how their characters have changed by the end of the story.

_____

_____

_____

_____

_____

_____

_____

The questions you have answered about 'Cow's Head' have tested your understanding of what happens in the story and also helped you to consider the techniques used by the storyteller. If you have already read and answered the questions about the story 'High and Lifted Up' in Chapter 6 (pages 54–59), you could now try the extended task on the next page, which asks you to write about both these stories in greater detail.

Extended task

Write a detailed comparison of the two stories 'High and Lifted Up' and 'Cow's Head'. In particular you should write about:

- the characters in the stories
- the descriptions of the background and weather
- who you think the audiences for them are
- the endings of each story and the lessons each one contains for the reader.

In your conclusion say which of the stories you enjoyed more and give reasons for your choice.

Plan your work in the space below and then write your answer on separate paper.

Writing task

Write the following parts of two different short stories:

a) the opening to a story containing mysterious happenings

b) the conclusion to a story dealing with events in the life of a happy and contented family.

In both pieces of writing you should concentrate on conveying the atmosphere through your descriptions. You should include **one character only** in each piece of writing.

Do **not** write complete stories.

Plan your work in the space below and then write your story parts on separate paper.

Exercise

Paragraphing

The sentences below make up a paragraph about the Amazon Basin, but they have been jumbled up and only Sentence 1 and Sentence 8 are in the correct position.

Unscramble the rest of the sentences and rewrite them as an ordered and logically constructed paragraph on separate paper. You do not need to change any of the wording – just the order of the sentences.

1   The Amazon rainforest gets its name from the Amazon River, the life force of the rainforest.

2   Sixteen per cent of all the world's river water flows through the Amazon delta.

3   127 billion litres of water flow into the Atlantic every minute, diluting the salinity of the ocean for more than 160 kilometres offshore.

4   Its drainage basin covers 7 050 000 square kilometres, and lies in the countries of Brazil, Columbia, Peru, Venezuela, Ecuador, Bolivia, and the three Guyanas.

5   The main river is about 6560 kilometres long.

6   It meets the Atlantic Ocean at Belem, Brazil.

7   The Amazon River begins in the Peruvian Andes, and winds its way east over the northern half of South America.

8   The Amazon rainforest watershed is home to the world's highest level of biodiversity.

Teacher comments

8 Poetry

Reading

This chapter looks at two different types of poem. The first two examples are lyrical poems on a similar topic, both of which provide food for thought. The third poem is an example of narrative verse.

Read the first two poems carefully and then answer the questions that follow the second one. Some of the words and phrases in the first poem have been explained for you.

Important Notice
Philip Waddell

World Wildlife Industries sadly announces
that we may soon have to close due to fierce
competition from Human Beings International.

Many of our famous products are already
unavailable including, to name but three, our *dodo*,
quagga and once healthy *passenger pigeon* lines.

> The dodo and passenger pigeon are extinct types of bird; quaggas were an ancient type of zebra, now also extinct.

Currently under threat are many of our
stock of mammals and fishes as well as
birds, reptiles, amphibians *and* insects.

But even now we could be helped to survive.
Work together with your parents and teachers

to find out how you could all help before it is too late.

And remember – without us and the products

of our other branch, World Vegetation Industries,
our world too might soon be without *your* company.

Let's work together to stay in business.

Mother Nature

Managing Director

The Last Wolf Speaks from the Zoo

Pie Corbett

By day
I hid in the ferns
pressed to the earth,
dressed in a coat
brown as turf.

Sunlight warmed
the patches where
my wolf pack once lay.

Day after day
childflesh spills past the wire;
they pause, point and stare –
I size them up –
glare back –
through thin red eyes.

Years back
my sister caught one –
cracked a finger –
left the childflesh
to scowl and howl.

The next day
they took my sister away.
But her smell stayed
trapped in the earth's spoor.
It took a full moon's span
for it to fade.

Now, alone,
I watch
and wait for her.

At night
the stars glisten.
I listen for the pack.
I sing to the moon.

I croon an ancient tune.
But she is muzzled
and cannot answer back.

Now answer these questions on 'Important Notice' and 'The Last Wolf Speaks from the Zoo'. You should try to use your own words as far as possible.

1   Explain as fully as you can what is being said in the opening three lines of 'Important Notice'. Who is speaking and what does the speaker represent?

_____

_____

_____

_____

_____

_____

2   What is implied by the statement 'Many of our famous products are already unavailable'?

_____

3   What or who has caused this unavailability? How are readers of the poem being asked to help?

_____

_____

4   In the second poem, where is the wolf and what is it referring to in the first eight lines of the poem?

_____

_____

5   What is meant by 'childflesh' and what happened when the wolves met childflesh 'years back'?

_____

_____

_____

6 Explain as fully as you can the thoughts and memories the wolf refers to in the final verses of the poem (from 'But her smell ...').

_____

_____

_____

_____

_____

_____

Extended task

Both of these poems contain a similar message. Write a comparison of the two in which you consider the similarities and differences between them. You should write about what the poets say and the words and language that they use. Which of the poems do you find most effective in communicating its message? Give reasons for your answer.

Plan your answer here.

Notes and quotations

Write your answer here.

The next poem is a narrative poem that tells a story set in ancient Greece about a competition between two sculptors. The ending makes us question the way we tend to make judgements before we see the whole picture.

Read the poem carefully and then answer the questions that follow. Some of the words and phrases in the poem have been explained for you.

The Statue
Henry Abbey

All bold, great actions that are seen too near,
Look rash and foolish to unthinking eyes;
But at a distance they at once appear
In their true grandeur: so let us be wise,
And not too soon our neighbour's deed malign,
Lest what seems crude should prove to be divine.

In Athens, when all learning centr'd there,
Men reared a column of surpassing height
In honour of *Minerva*, wise and fair;   Greek goddess of wisdom
And on the top, which dwindled to the sight,
A statue of the goddess was to stand,
That wisdom might be known to all the land.

And he who, with the beauty in his heart,
Seeking in faultless work immortal youth,
Would mould this statue with the finest art,
Making the wintry marble glow with truth,
Should gain the prize: two sculptors sought the fame –
The prize they craved was an enduring name.

Alcamenes soon carved his little best;   Phidias and Alcamenes
But *Phidias*, beneath a dazzling thought   were rival sculptors in
That like a bright sun in a cloudless west   ancient Greece 2500 years
Lighted his wide, great soul, with pure love wrought   ago. Alcamenes had been
A statue, and its changeless face of stone   a student of Phidias.
With calm, far-sighted wisdom towered and shone.

Then to be judged the labours were unveiled;
But, at the marble thought, that by degrees
Of hardship Phidias cut, the people railed.
'The lines are coarse, the form too large,' said these;
'And he who sends this rough result of haste
Sends scorn, and offers insult to our taste.'

Alcamenes' praised work was lifted high
Upon the column, ready for the prize;
But it appeared too small against the sky,
And lacked proportion to uplooking eyes;
So it was quickly lowered and put aside,
And the scorned thought was mounted to be tried.

Surprise swept o'er the faces of the crowd,
And changed them as a sudden breeze may change
A field of fickle grass, and long and loud
The mingled shouts to see a sight so strange.
The statue stood completed in its place,
Each coarse line melted to a line of grace.

Now answer these questions. You should try to use your own words in your answers as much as possible.

1   Explain the meaning of the following words and phrases as used in the poem:

a) malign _____

b) surpassing _____

c) dwindled to the sight _____

d) enduring _____

e) the people railed _____

f) proportion _____

g) fickle _____

2   Where was it intended that the statue of Minerva should be placed?

_____

3   Explain, using your own words, what the two sculptors hoped to gain from their work.

_____

_____

4 By referring closely to the poet's choice of words and his use of similes and metaphors in verse 4, explain how he presents Phidias as a better sculptor than Alcamenes.

_____

_____

_____

5 Explain fully why the people at first criticised the sculpture produced by Phidias.

_____

_____

6 What proved to be the failing with Alcamenes' sculpture?

_____

_____

7 Re-read the first verse of the poem and then explain as fully as you can how the point that it makes is illustrated by the rest of the poem.

_____

_____

_____

_____

Writing task

Think of a topic about which you have strong feelings. Using the poems 'Important Notice' and 'The Last Wolf Speaks from the Zoo' as a starting point, try to write either a poem or a prose description that makes a powerful appeal to people in your age group in order to make them aware of your concerns.

Plan your work in the space below and then write your answer on separate paper.

_____

_____

_____

_____

_____

_____

_____

_____

_____

_____

_____

_____

_____

Exercises

Vocabulary: synonyms

The three words in each question below all have similar meanings but are not always interchangeable. Write sentences containing each of the words in order to illustrate their different shades of meaning.

1 a) angry: _____

_____

b) annoyed: _____

_____

c) furious: _____

_____

2 a) eat: _____

_____

b) devour: _____

_____

c) graze: _____

_____

3 a) hardworking: _____

_____

b) persevering: _____

_____

c) thorough: _____

_____

4 a) happy: _____

_____

b) delighted: _____

_____

c) pleased: _____

_____

5 **a)** lonely: _____

_____

b) isolated: _____

_____

c) solitary: _____

_____

6 **a)** rude: _____

_____

b) inconsiderate: _____

_____

c) cheeky: _____

_____

7 **a)** run: _____

_____

b) rush: _____

_____

c) hasten: _____

_____

8 a) small: _____

_____

b) tiny: _____

_____

c) narrow: _____

_____

9 a) think: _____

_____

b) believe: _____

_____

c) suspect: _____

_____

10 a) tired: _____

_____

b) exhausted: _____

_____

c) overworked: _____

_____

Figurative language: similes and metaphors

1   All the following sentences use figurative language and contain either a
simile, a **metaphor** or both.

Identify the figurative language in each sentence by writing either **S** (for a simile),
M (for a metaphor) or both in the box.

a) The trees swayed in the breeze like elegant dancers.

b) We were blanketed in the darkness of the night.

c) He jumped from rock to rock as if he was a mountain goat.

d) The leaden weight of my homework assignment weighed
me down.

e) The heavy walls of clouds guarded the sun.

f) The frost like a white crust held the earth in its iron grasp.

g) The howling of the traffic grated my eardrums.

h) The stairs groaned under my tread as if they were in pain.

i) The memory of the dream was like toothache in my brain
that would not go away.

j) The moon was a ghostly galleon tossed upon the clouds.

2   Give an example of a simile and a metaphor for the following:

a) An empty classroom

Simile: _____

Metaphor: _____

b) A thunderstorm

Simile: _____

Metaphor: _____

   c) The way a giraffe moves

     Simile: _____

     Metaphor: _____

   d) The sound of the crowd at a football game

     Simile: _____

     Metaphor: _____

   e) A gentle piece of music

     Simile: _____

     Metaphor: _____

Teacher comments